90 AT 90

90 INNER ADVENTURES ON THE ROAD TO 90

KENNETH J. DALE

To order additional copies of this book, contact:
Xlibris
1-888-795-4274
www.Xlibris.com
Orders@Xlibris.com
727008

TABLE OF CONTENTS

PREFACE

I have been writing essays and journals all my life. Writing helps me to clarify and deepen my understanding and experience of faith and life. It is my sincere hope that sharing my wrestling on some important issues of faith will be of help to others, especially to those who have one foot in the Christian tradition and one foot wavering where to step next.

I think there are many in the church today who fit this description, often because they fail to see the relevance of traditional statements of faith to our contemporary context, attuned as it is, to scientific answers for all of life's issues.

It is my goal to seek new approaches in the struggle to find answers to some of these issues related to the Christian concept of God and the presence of God in human life. Hopefully, some of these ideas that I have found meaningful might be helpful also to you as you seek bridges between your questions and what I believe to be the essence of Christian faith.

With this goal in mind, I have published *A Seeker's Journal: Questioning Tradition, Strengthening Faith* 2003 (also translated into Japanese), and *A Mosaic of Musings: Daily Thoughts for People on the Way (*2010). Now, with this little book, no doubt my last, I again wish to dialogue with my readers about a few important issues of faith and life.

The reader will soon discover that 90 is a significant number for me at this time. The 90 years of life God has granted me are reflected in the 9 chapters, which together contain 90 jottings or mini-essays that constitute this book. These have been written from time to time over a period of years, so the reader cannot always expect logical coherence in content.

Kenneth J. Dale
Pilgrim Place, Claremont, CA
March 3, 2016

I

Seeking God

The first two chapters are devoted to the subject of God-- God, whom no human being has ever seen, yet the one whom people of all times and places have sought. Who is this God?

1

Where *spirit* and *Spirit* meet

Imagine the absurdity of the human race, through all times and places around this globe, worshiping a god, or God. Almost all civilizations have had a religious element whereby people reverenced a Being one has never seen! How irrational! But the fact that religion and belief in an invisible Being is so universal tells me that it must not be absurd after all.

How is it that the human race is compelled to such belief and religious practice? Is it not because we experience something invisible and yet undeniably real within ourselves? Stop and think: Life as such is not visible. Thought, will, feelings are undeniably a part of our daily experience, yet they are invisible. So it is with the divine Reality.

All this strengthens my faith. When I feel God is nowhere to be found, I remember my own spirit, for I know absolutely that I am not just a hunk of flesh; I am aware of the invisible realities that compose my heart, and aware of what Marcus Borg calls the "More" which makes me me! Linking *spirit* with *Spirit* in this way is helpful in making faith plausible and real for me.

2

The lure that makes us seekers

"I am the Lord your God, you shall have no other gods before me," the first of the great Ten Commandments given by Moses, lays out the perspective, the landscape of true religion for the Abrahamic faith--Jews, Christians and Muslims: There is a God, and this God is one, and is invisible, and longs for our complete allegiance.

Yet this God, being invisible and without "scientific" validation, is, by that God's very nature, impossible to describe, much less to define. So why believe in such an entity?

The writers of the Psalms of the Old Testament often speak of *seeking* God. I empathize with that. My life has been a constant search. We would not seek unless something is beyond us, luring us to search on and on. We begin to experience the divine in the act of seeking. The joy is in the journey!

I sometimes feel that my "calling" is to focus my theological pondering on the First Article of the traditional creeds, i.e., on God the Creator. I feel drawn to understand God in a more philosophical way than those who focus on the Second Article—Jesus and redemption. These folks are dealing with history. First Article folks are not.

From my experience in the Lutheran Church, it seems we have a strong tendency to concentrate on the Second Article ("I believe in Jesus Christ..."). When this is taken to the extreme, Christian faith becomes a kind of "Jesusology," which is not sufficiently inclusive of the mystery of the divine nature.

3

Meeting God—in my body!

I seek eagerly for peace with God, the inscrutable One in the midst of all life's experiences, but I find there is a huge gap between intellectual "solutions" and the deeper gut-level experience of finding a joyful peace-filled faith and commitment. But I'm coming to see God more and more as the sum total of all existence, as the cause and fount of my existence, as well as that of the universe. God is not the emperor of the universe, but is the breath of life, the energy in all things, all events, that by which everything exists.

Where can I meet this God? If the material/spiritual world is not something separate from God but is the very place and stuff where God is, then it follows that to honor God and hallow his name I should not try to concentrate on some celestial Being or on spirituality as such, but rather focus on the things close around me, on the work I am doing, and not least on my own body. For if I don't meet God there, I meet God nowhere!

If God's Spirit is not embodied in *my body*, it is not a reality for me at all. As I prayed today I had a sense that the Spirit needed a vessel to give form to the formless, and my physical self was the only vessel available. Significantly, St. Paul called our body "the temple of the Holy Spirit."

How thankful I am for this wonderful body, still in basically good condition after 90 years! I want to be aware of the Holy One in this body today!

4

The Kingdom of God is where?

Where is heaven and the "Kingdom of Heaven" (synonymous with Kingdom of God)? Jesus said, "The Kingdom of Heaven is within you," and "I am with you always," and "I in them and they in me," etc. It makes Jesus' understanding of God and the Spirit very much like the panentheistic view of God—the divine Spirit in everything, and everything in the divine.

The implication is that there is no God "out there" occasionally impinging on members of the human race, on human history, or on nature and the climate, etc. as in traditional theism.

Remember the story of Elijah, where it is written (I Kings 19) that he wanted the Lord to visit him? First there was a powerful wind that shattered the rock, but the Lord was not in the wind; then a great earthquake, then a fire, but the Lord was not in any of these. But finally there came a gentle whisper, and that was the revelation he had been waiting for.

This whole image is telling us that God is not "out there" as some objective phenomenon, but is "in here," immanent in my life, hiding in the structure of my *self*, and your *self*.

5

Science enhances religion

Science is a great friend and supplement to religion. Ancient Judaism believed in God "the Maker of Heaven and Earth," but modern science has discovered and named the intricate content of, and described the specifics of, "heaven and earth" in a way never before known—cells, DNA, atoms, quarks, galaxies, and on and on—and has also identified the evolutionary process of the inhabited world. Thanks to these investigations into the marvelous nature of "heaven and earth" by science, our appreciation of the created universe grows richer and our praise to the Creator rises higher!

The discrepancy between the description of creation according to science and the description according to the first chapters of Genesis is, of course, a critical issue for those in the fundamentalist tradition. I myself find no discrepancy whatsoever because the Bible does not pretend to be a book of science. The opening chapters of Genesis are a great poem of the ancient Hebrew people, visualizing their faith in a living God whom they saw as active in the material universe from the very beginning of time.

6

Is there a right system of theology?

I compulsively look for the *right system* for thinking about God and religious matters. Both those words lead me off course. Since God is unknowable, it is impossible to arrange experiences and thoughts of God into a *system*; i.e., an intellectual framework that necessarily establishes a structure for the object we are dealing with. If we conclude that true religion centered on the true God is by nature unsystematic, what does that mean for academic theology?

And the word *right* is definitely inappropriate. Nobody knows what is right. There is no human authority to determine what is right, and no divine authority because each person hears a different "divine" message in his or her conscience.

I am aware that what I have just said is in direct contradiction to a fundamentalist view of the Bible. For fundamentalists, the Bible is always right; the Bible has divine authority; the Bible has all the answers. For the moment we must simply admit that there is a huge gap in religious understanding between non-fundamentalists and fundamentalists, who believe in an absolute book.

7

God is not "in control"

I see that God does not control the world and human life. It runs by itself, producing good events and bad events. I believe that this is simply the way the universe is created. So we are on the wrong track to thank God for the good things that happen, and turn from God when bad things happen.

And we are also on the wrong track to think that God is, therefore, absent from the world, from our lives. I believe God is present in all things of creation, always. God is here suffering with us in our sadness, and taking delight in what we delight in.

And this infuses life with meaning, and with a great stability. Without this ineffable comfort we are lonely and incomplete. The biblical answer to this human situation is the belief that we are created in the "image of God," which leaves us with a very basic existential longing to return to our Source, to live with and for our Parent. As St. Augustine said, "Our hearts are restless until they rest in Thee."

8

We need an integrating center

For me to be a fully functioning human being I need an integrating center. Without that I disintegrate into fragments, such as fragments of body, of reasoning, of imagination, of conceit, of an array of emotions, and so forth. My *self* can be this integrating center, but even that self can easily become dysfunctional when it is torn with the conflicts of the many fragments, the many pieces of the jig-saw puzzle making up a *life*.

Here is where I find the need for something or someone bigger than all these human elements, something to be a source of all the fragments, and a goal toward which all the fragments can move. I call that *God*.

Likewise, the world, the universe, needs an integrating center to make sense of the myriad of fragmented parts—disparate ethnic groups, the human struggle with nature, the amazing findings of modern science, and so forth. How can we make sense of all these fragments of existence without some kind of integrating center, the center that I call God?

9

The unitive approach

I increasingly appreciate Richard Rohr's daily meditations online. His emphasis is on the unity of all things—material and spiritual, heaven and earth, divine and human. It is because of the Incarnation that we know this, for the existence of Jesus, who was the "son of man" and the "son of God," is a kind of archetype of the way God always works in the world. That is, God is enfleshed in surprising ways within material (including human) things.

Everything in my experience is of God. Nothing is hidden. God is already in everything of nature and in the whole human phenomenon. That doesn't mean we live in constant fear of this everywhere-present God—just the opposite! Some have called God the *Totality of Reality* (Dowd, *Thank God for Evolution*). In this there is great freedom—freedom from anxiety, shame, fear. In this there is also great joy!

10

"How not to see God"

These words, a bit startling, were part of the title of a lecture at All Saints Church in 2015. The full title is "Modern Atheism and How Not to See God." The majority of church goers are content with the traditional status quo in both teaching and practice within the church.

But there is turmoil in theological circles over notions of God, nature, and the universe. Here is the gist of the promotional paragraph following the above lecture title: Modern Christians should not work harder to see God and define God. Instead, we need strategies for abiding within God's *invisibility* more faithfully. This lecture shares how leading intellectuals are rethinking the being of God.

Karen Armstrong finds that what unites sincere people of all religions is *compassion.* I have a friend who goes a step further to say that if compassion is supreme in our—and all— religions, what role does God have to play? If the essence of religious faith is love, and if we live by love, then there is really no need for assuming that someone or something called God exists outside of the reality of love itself. Those are radical words.

But before dismissing them, I feel these concepts should be valued as a bridge which might bring young people into a meaningful dialogue about religion in life. We are aware that most of the younger generation, especially those involved in higher education, are already out on the edge of any religion at all. We need to be open to new approaches to old issues. We need to rethink our image of God.

II

God, the Inscrutable One

We cannot describe or know God fully, since God is an inscrutable mystery.

11

Mystery reconciled with simplicity?

The vexing question of the personal God! Panentheistic concepts such as Process Theology proffers, answer most of my questions but do not satisfactorily answer how a God who is in everything and everyone can at the same time be personal. The personal element throws us back into the traditional concepts of a theistic, benevolent *Being.*

But if God is truly the Ultimate Reality, the nature of that God is an utter mystery. All agree God cannot be defined or confined, so why not then call God the Mystery, and honor and worship the Mystery? And the decisive point of the Mystery is just this—that at the same time this Mystery is universally present in all reality, it is also a personal spirit that imbues all personal spirits, of which I am one!

"Your God is too small!" is one "solution" offered to those who try to pin down the nature of God. The implication is that our notion of God tries to describe the indescribable, confine the unconfinable, understand what will always remain a vast mystery.

Yet, Jesus simply called this One his Father, and he used the intimate word for father, "Abba," which has the feel of the English "Papa." These things don't blend! I pray for the Spirit's gift of clarity, lest I spend my last days in the anxiety of yearning to know the unknowable.

12

Old images have to go!

While struggling with questions of the existence and nature of God, I had an ah-ha! moment which showed me decisively that we *must* totally get rid of that image of God as Someone "up there"—the image that has been bred into me for a life-time! I realized that if God is in the category of "someone up there," such a god is not the Christian God at all, but simply another god, and to worship that one is equal to worshiping an idol.

God's existence is far more incomprehensible than such an image suggests. God is somehow mysteriously in, with and under the whole of creation, including nature and humanity. God is the very Energy of Life. God is the Other, the More, as Marcus Borg often says, in the midst of every part of the natural processes, including the human birth and death cycle. But how hard it is to erase the old images!

When we believe that God is not *a being* among other beings, but truly the fullness of Reality, the Totality of the Universe, we possess a great security and relief, and at the same time a renewed sense of responsibility.

For nobody is standing "out there" either judging or helping me. The universe simultaneously operates *on its own* and *in God*. But that does not mean God controls the universe. God is, rather, the dynamic process of development of this evolving universe, including an evolving moral humankind, for which we share responsibility.

13

There is a larger dimension

To believe in God is to recognize there are broader parameters to my existence than my birth and my death, that there are broader parameters to history than historians and archaeologists together can imagine, that there are broader parameters to the universe than what current telescopes reveal to us. And no one knows what larger dimension that comes after death might be. To me God is the *infinite* dimension, and also the *intimate* dimension that permeates and enlivens all the dimensions of our lives and of the universe.

Many can live without this larger dimension in their experience, but as for me, I find it unbearably lonely not to be connected with that larger Other, not to hear the still small voice that surprises me with grace, not to hang on to hope for a glimpse—or an eternity—of another realm of unspeakable peace, beauty and power. Idle dreaming? Maybe so, maybe not.

14

The perplexing Trinity—and more

The Trinity—God as Father, Son and Holy Spirit—is a perplexing and confusing Christian doctrine to many—most?—people. However, in essence, to me it is simply an acknowledgement of three experiences of the Inscrutable One: "The Father" is that understanding of God as the philosophical concept of creative power which gives birth to our universe, the awesome Creative Process, the Mystery of the "more than nature."

"The Son" is understanding God through the life of the historical person of Jesus. Through his life, teachings, death and resurrection he demonstrated the essence of his Father's character, viz., compassion for the world, and he taught that the same compassion should mark our behavior.

The "Holy Spirit" is understanding God as an existential energy experienced in personal awareness. This divine spiritual energy makes the character of the Father and the Son available to and efficacious in every human being

These three may be called by different nomenclature—that makes no difference. But all three of these aspects of the divine being are equally important in fulfilling our longing and need for a God that "fills all in all."

We can best point to what we believe is the nature of God through the use of analogies and metaphors rather than reasoning. For instance, *life* and *light* are both everyday phenomena, yet both are actually mysterious realities, without which no one can survive. It is no wonder they have been used even in the Scriptures as metaphors—"I am the light of the world;" "I am the way, the truth and the life;" etc. Maybe they are more than metaphors. Maybe God *is* life. I ponder that one often.

15

The God color

Teilhard de Chardin's theme in *The Divine Milieu* is that God is in everything; it is our responsibility to "divinize" the world. But he is no idealist. He says, "Everything is God, yet everything is dust." Perhaps the TV screen is an analogy: Sometimes when something goes wrong, color vanishes from the screen and the picture turns black and white. How dull and uninteresting it looks--like dust and chalk. But when color returns to the screen, everything becomes vibrant and alive. That is analogous to the transforming power of the divine Spirit that gives new, vibrant color and meaning to our experience.

We all have similar daily experiences, but we see them through different lenses. Some people wear glasses that can see God in everything. They see everything as beautiful, or exciting, or having profound meaning. When those glasses are removed, we see only a drab, cold, depressing world.

16

God as "*isness*"

I wonder if we should think about God in this way: God is not only in everything that is, but God is the very *isness* of the world. The marvel is that the universe exists at all, that you and I exist. All that exists, all life, all nature is precious, marvelously made and gifted to us.

What does this insight say about an appropriate religious response on our part? It says that our proper posture is to be grateful for everything, because all that *is*, is a gift, it's not our doing at all. It behooves us to care for all that exists, to respect it, to devote our lives to enhancing it, using it with care, protecting it where it is fragile. Be aware! Give thanks! Take care! might be a summary of the Christian's life.

But the question might legitimately be asked, Then what is the difference between this concept of God and the pantheistic concept, in which anything can be considered a god and worshipped? The Judaeo-Christian tradition answers this question with the belief in *creation*.

The very first words of the Hebrew Bible are, "In the beginning God created…." Likewise the first words of the Gospel of John in the New Testament are, "In the beginning was the Word (*logos*)…. Through him (*logos*) all things were made."

In Christian thought the *Creating Spirit* and *created matter* are not identical. Although one cannot exist apart from the other, they are still not the same. Only the one invisible Creating Spirit, and never any part of created matter is worthy of our ultimate worship.

17

The Holy Father

The words of the so-called Lord's Prayer give us a clue about our proper relationship to God. In this prayer we don't ask God for specific personal things; we don't thank God for such specific things. It does not visualize God as a Santa Claus who hands out gifts and blessings to some and not to others. This makes a mockery of the one who deserves the title "God." God is far beyond such a gift-giver.

Recall the first sentence of the Lord's Prayer: "Hallowed be thy name." This strange sentence reminds us that God is "holy" (hallowed)—different from anything else in the world, wholly "Other." Therefore our proper response to God is not thanks for particulars, but a reminder to ourselves that the very existence of the universe is what we should be grateful for. The mystery of the existence of the universe and the mystery of the existence of my own selfhood—these should call forth, not thanks (God doesn't need our thank-you's), so much as awe and adoration.

The word "hallowed" points to the unfathomable, holy mystery of existence. If that is so, how could the word "Father" be used in the same context!? A father is human, personal, intimate! This is the paradox at the root of the Christian understanding of God.

18

Two metaphors pointing to God

How did Jesus understand God? If we knew that, it should be a clue for the way we understand God. At this point the prayer which he taught his followers ("the Lord's Prayer") is, although cloaked in simplicity, profoundly enlightening. He said, "Our Father who is in heaven." This appellation has two profound meanings, cloaked in figures of speech. 1) "Father" is of course not a literal father, so it is a metaphor—of what? Can we say it is a metaphor of One who is a progenitor, who is personal, and who is a loving provider? This alone provides a basic Christian understanding of God's nature.

2) "Who is in heaven"—another metaphor, because nobody knows what or where heaven really is. What it does obviously mean is some form of existence different—utterly different—than earth and all we know about the physical universe. If God is "in heaven," that God's existence is unlike any image we may have in our minds, and is indeed beyond all human imagination. In fact, any of the beautiful images of heaven we hear described, especially at funerals, may be closer to idolatry than reality. None of the words about heaven found in the Bible claim to be factual descriptions.

19

"God so loved the world..."

This is a kind of universally accepted key sentence of the whole Bible (John 3:16). We take it for granted and even children glibly recite it. But have you ever asked, Why does God love the world? Why should God love the world? That of course is unanswerable, but it is another way of saying that the powerful energy which brought the universe—including the human family—into being is a *benevolent* energy. "God is love" is one of the most provocative sentences in the New Testament. It is the overwhelming insight that we live in a *benevolent universe*. In church language we call this *grace,* and speak of God as a *gracious* God. This grace, this oceanic love, is the constant source of hope for all living beings, and for me

III

The Way of Jesus Christ

Jesus Christ is the One in whom mystery and history converge.
What is the significance for us of his life and his death?

20

To "believe in Jesus" means....

"Believe in Jesus and be saved," is a key phrase for traditional Christian evangelists. But it is more of a stumbling block than a saving grace to many, including myself. So what are we trying to say when we say, "Believe in Jesus"? Is it something like this? Jesus claimed to have, and demonstrated that he had, special divine power prompting him to do "mighty works." Put in the simplest terms, we believe God was working through this man Jesus in a special way.

That is the meaning of the whole concept of Incarnation—the divine incarnated in human flesh. Another way of saying this is to say Jesus was a man who had left his ego behind and was completely open to the spirit of God living and working in him.

To believe in Jesus is to believe in this dramatically exciting possibility, not just in Jesus, but in all people—incarnation! God in us, God working through us, God's presence in all open hearts and minds.

And Jesus' mighty works were always manifestations of loving compassion. That exposes the character of the divine power working in him. In this way Jesus showed us that we can, in spite of suffering, experience the universe as essentially benevolent.

The words I have used here are different from the traditional Christian terminology of "Trinity," "Son of God and Son of Man," "Savior of the world," and so forth. Indeed they might seem heretical to some ears. But I am only trying to put a basic experience of the Holy One into fresh terms that hopefully make sense to some for whom the traditional terminology does not make sense.

21

When mystery and history meet

Traditional Christian theology says that Jesus was both divine and human. As such, Jesus was a part of history. But the divine is a mystery. So how can "both divine and human" make sense, when those two represent entirely different worlds—the world of mystery and the world of history?

This is an age-old dilemma with no solution. Instead of trying to define the Incarnation with rational statements, I think it is better simply to say, In Jesus the Mystery became Reality. The *how* of that statement must remain forever a puzzle.

22

Who was/is Jesus?

For a long time I have focused on concepts and experiences of *God* in my theological and devotional search. But should not the focus be on Jesus, the Christ? All people seek after God in some fashion, but for Christians, it is that mystery man, Jesus Christ, who is the center of our faith.

How should we understand the Christ? In John's Gospel Jesus is identified with *light*, and the light is identified with *right*, and darkness with wrong and evil. So should we not identify Christ with the *right way of life* that he taught, and lived and died for, namely, the way of sacrificial love. And that is different from simply identifying him as a person named Jesus and adoring that person. If a line, ambiguous though it might be, can be drawn between "Jesus" and "Jesus' way of life," then I would say that to "believe in Jesus" means to "believe in Jesus' way of life" and to appropriate that way for ourselves.

23

"Panentheism"

On this Easter eve I was given this insight: We say the post-resurrection Christ is active in the world—how can we image that? The *logos*—the Word that was with God, was God became flesh—God's expression in creation, in history and finally through Jesus (Read the first chapter of John). That Word is still coming in the form of Christ alive in the world, even though his contemporaries thought they had done away with him.

Process Theology speaks about God in terms of "Panentheism," ("all-in-God"), which says that God is in everything, everything is in God, or, the Cosmic Christ is in everything, everything is in the cosmic Christ.

Is not this line of thought consonant with the *logos* concept, which the Gospel of John equates with God? John says the *logos*, as the expression of the otherwise incomprehensible God, was the instrument of creation, finally becoming human flesh, and finally, after the resurrection, becoming the Spirit who is everywhere present—the "cosmic Christ."

Also recall Paul's words, "Christ *in you*.... For me *to live is Christ*.... etc." Is not St. Paul here expressing the same essence as implied in the more modern phrase, "panentheism," i.e., the divine Spirit, the Cosmic Christ, the eternal Logos *in us?*

24

I am the way

Let's face it, the statement of Jesus which so often becomes problematic in inter-faith dialogues, viz., "I am the way, the truth and the life; no one comes to the Father but by me," does give Christians pause before they devote themselves to good feelings about other religions. But there is much to be said about this problematic sentence. An interpretation which is very meaningful to me runs like this:

The accent is not on "I" in this sentence, but on "way, truth, life," the descriptive or the identity of "I." That is to say, finding the Father is not so much through *Jesus* as one person out of countless other religious "saviors," but on Jesus' *way of living, his truth*, i.e., true or right thinking and acting totally open to and rooted in God, a life completely expressing the love of God for the world. This is what identified the person of Jesus. Living in these truths, living open to and rooted in the divine love, this is what constitutes the way to God.

What to some is the "slippery slope" statement which follows, namely, that there is no theological necessity to confine this *way* to Jesus of Nazareth. We do not know the mind of God; we do not dictate God's loving purposes and plans for the human race.

25

The most unique words in Scripture

Perhaps the most unique words of the entire Bible, or at least of the words of Jesus, are: "This is my body, take and eat…this is my blood, take and drink." Has any other sage or saint or self-acclaimed god in all history said such outrageous words as these? "Eat my body, drink my blood!!" But with these word, that is, the stance of pouring out himself for others. At the end he gave substance, gave a universal, archetypal meaning to this testimony by actually sacrificing his own life.

So, on that last night before his death—and this is the part so hard to take that we like to overlook it—he made an indelible impression during that last supper that what he was about to do was indeed giving himself for them *so they could give themselves for others.* Jesus wanted his followers to be so empowered by and imbued with this spirit that he expressed it with that powerful, astonishing metaphor—"Embrace me, let me become part of you, one with you—eat me! Let the substance of my life become the substance of your life!"

26

This is my body...

These final words of Jesus, we say, are God giving himself for humankind in Jesus' self-giving life and death. But who is the God who gives himself for us? We no longer see God as a Being "out there" who decides to send his Son into the world to die on a cross to save the world. Rather, we see God in everything, we see the whole universe as God's Body. With that understanding of God, how do we see the sacramental act of Christ?

Think of it this way: In creation God gives the divine Self to the world, to us. All of nature, all of history—*all* is an act of grace, love, self-giving. Everything is gift! All of creation is a sacramental act— the sacred within the profane, the spiritual within the material, the holy in everything. The *crowning* gift was the act of Christ giving his life on the cross, saying "This is my body broken for you."

All we can do is be grateful and humble before these immeasurable gifts of grace as we partake of "the bread and wine made holy" and remember the words, "...given *for you*."

27

The dynamic of sacrifice in ritual

The Christian church holds the person and work of Jesus, climaxing in the cross experience (his suffering, death and resurrection), at its center. I have always been intrigued by the dynamics of Christian "theories of atonement," which attempt to explain how this work of Christ affects us ordinary folks. Let's discuss that for a minute.

The perpetrator of wrong feels guilty. The victim of wrong feels resentful. How can restitution and reconciliation take place? The perpetrator must give up something of his own, give a gift of value as a token of remorse and repentance. The victim has to give up his pride and status by saying, "You've wounded me and that hurts, but I will intentionally put the hurt behind me, forget about it, forgive you, so we can be reconciled."

Since ancient times, religious ritual recognized that we sin against God by disobeying the moral order, hurting God when we hurt our neighbor. So from ancient times the Jewish custom was to give something of value—often a valuable animal—as a gift to God, believing that when God sees this genuine remorse he accepts human repentance and forgives the sin.

Then, as we shall see in the next reading, comes something new!

28

The meaning of "the new covenant"

If what is written above was the pre-Christian Jewish dynamic of forgiveness, what is the Christian answer to the problem of guilt and reconciliation? The Anselm theory says that Jesus was the sacrifice offered for the whole human race, and God saw this sacrifice, accepted it and so God can forgive sin "for Jesus' sake."

But that is not really a *new* covenant/arrangement between God and man at all. Jesus' new way says, "I have come to do your will." And in the doing of God's will through the actions and teachings of his whole ministry, he got killed. His death was inevitable because human darkness is such that it could not accept the perfect life of Jesus, consistently putting compassion for human needs before religious ritual and institutional survival, to the consternation of the traditionalists of his day.

So, in this whole process we see the cross as the highest mark of the sacrifice of the divine One for humankind. The old system has been overthrown. The human offering of sacrifice in order to be forgiven of sin is no longer needed; we understand at last that it's all taken care of already in the very nature of divine love.

So is nothing required of us? Yes, something is required—not an appeasement sacrifice, but rather answering the call of this Jesus to follow him, to follow his way of sacrificing everything in order to be open and obedient to the God of love, standing up for right and just decisions, no matter what the cost.

29

"He carried our sorrows"

The words of Isaiah, "He carried our sorrows; he bore our sins," describes Jesus' whole life on earth. He completely identified with human suffering, and poignantly suffered himself. That is Incarnation. That is also Redemption, understood not so much as a one-time act on the cross, but as a lifetime of sacrificing himself in service to others. *That* is the unconditional love of God that forgives and reconciles us. And we who follow Jesus are called to do likewise—constantly bear each other's burdens.

30

What kind of God?

Sometimes we hear the thought-provoking statement, "To believe in God is not as important as to follow Jesus." True, one doesn't even have to be religious to believe in the existence of a God, the originating and empowering Force in all creation. Such a belief comes closer to philosophy than religion.

So what is the essential element in "believing in God" for Christians? Is it not to hold the conviction and the hope that God is like Jesus? As Christians, who believe that somehow Jesus represented God to us, we believe that this empowering Force in all creation is a benevolent Power, a loving Presence, always seeking the highest good for everyone and everything. Jesus stood for compassion and love in all his ways and works, claiming that he was doing the work of God. Jesus opened the window so we can see and breathe in a benevolent universe! There is hope and joy in that!

IV

"What Are Human Beings, That Thou art Mindful of Them?"

We believe God is good, so why is there so much evil in the world, and in us? We daily experience sin in our lives, but also experience the grace of a "benevolent universe."

31

Our interior geography

It occurs to me that we need to pay attention to the astonishingly complex interior geography of our inner life. What is that? I would say it is the delicate movement of thought, feeling, intuition, the voice of conscience, moral sensitivity, and also a mysterious "X-factor" which we experience as the prompting of the Holy Spirit of God.

Some people are more in touch with this interior geography than others. Some are more capable of maneuvering in a positive route through the complexities than others. Some despise this inner life by completely neglecting it—at their own loss. All of us are more attentive to this interiority at certain times, and less at other times. It takes considerable energy to be alert to this inner road map. I often fail, but when I take time to watch the compass carefully, the ensuing trip is worth it.

St. Paul had a deep struggle between flesh and spirit ("Nothing good dwells in my flesh, for I can will what is right but cannot do it." (Romans 7.18). I believe that this struggle is basically not with so-called "fleshly lusts," or even with specific evil deeds. For me, it is rather the persistent difficulty I experience in failing to acknowledge the presence of God in our midst, in nature, in myself.

My tendency is to neglect that stance of mindfulness of and openness to the divine presence which knocks gently at my door. But I disregard this knock to my own detriment. This natural tendency to let myself get submerged in material things and immediate satisfaction is my "original sin." I think this is what Paul called the "flesh" with which he struggled.

32

Do I sin against *God?*

I have a sense that all things in the world comprise a grand, harmonious unity—nature and humanity all together. I am a part of it. What a wonderful world! What a wonderful life!

But I continually do things that are disruptive of that harmony—disrupting harmonious human relations by putting self above all others, disrupting the wholesomeness of nature by contaminating air and water—the basic elements for human health. These actions destroy the grand harmonious whole. This is what we call sin. And I am guilty of these things every day. It is sin against the One who holds this whole together. That's why, as Jesus taught, we pray to God as well as to our neighbor, "Forgive us our sin."

It is obvious that we need to forgive each other because we wrong each other in so many ways. But without this understanding of sin, asking *God* for forgiveness does not make much sense.

33

Adam and Eve and the apple

How about this interpretation of the "Fall" of Adam and Eve in the garden (Genesis 1): God might be portrayed as giving the apple as something beautiful to look at and to enjoy. But human beings did not appreciate it; they could not defer their wants; they merely *consumed it!* That started the "slippery slope" downward!

We are a shamefully greedy consumer society. We don't enjoy, appreciate, care for the things of nature; we don't ration out and appropriately defer the use of resources. Our selfish practice is to use them to satisfy our immediate desires, to reap the harvest without returning anything to the soil for the sake of the next generation, or to pollute the air and water with no thought of how precious clean air and water are. We use "the apple" as an economic tool, just to make money from buying and selling it!

34

At odds with myself

If the Spirit of God is truly *in me,* and if the Spirit of God is love, then I too am filled with compassionate love for people and the earth. For God is the Love that makes the world go round, the Spirit of Love which presses on me to live in and by that love.

But then the paradox strikes me in the face: I am *not* full of compassionate love. Why? Because I exist in an animal body, and as animal my primary instinct is self-preservation, and this is what puts my body and spirit in perennial conflict. This is the human dilemma: we want to live as God wills, but we can't. With St. Paul (Rom. 7) we cry out in anguish, "Why do I always do what I don't will to do!"

Not following our true nature—the way of creativity and love, i.e., the "image of God"—this is being at odds with our true self. There arises a gap between what we're meant to be, our highest self, and the way of self-centeredness via our animal instincts and desires. This is what we call sin—an inner profound gap between what we could and should be and what we actually are.

I take this to be the meaning of the Christian notion of the "Fall" which has arisen in the context of the story of Adam and Eve in the garden of Eden found in the first three chapters of the first book of the Bible (Genesis). The Eden story dramatizes human suffering as punishment from God for disobedience to the divine instruction. But the God we disobey is not an autocrat standing "out there" somewhere. We see this as a story (some call it myth) which puts into a vivid narrative that which is in reality an inner struggle.

35

"Let the weeds grow until harvest"

In Matt. 13 there is a parable of weeds being sown with the good seed. The harvester says, "Don't try to separate out the weeds now because you'll also destroy the good grain. Leave them both until harvest time." Good and bad are often the front and back side of the same phenomenon—and also the same person, like myself. To destroy the bad would be to destroy too much of human experience, which is a confusing mixture of good and evil.

Look at some obvious examples close to home: the aggressive person gets things done—good! But that aggressive person often tramples on others, hurts others' feelings—not so good! Or on the social scale, a developed society builds magnificent public facilities—good! But it's usually at the expense of low-paid workers living in poverty—not good! We wage war to protect our freedom—good! But that war cruelly kills countless persons, who, we tend to forget, are as much "children of God" as we are—not good!

So, tragically, human existence must continue in the context of this constant but ironical mix of good and evil in us and in society. This is the reality that gives us a hope for eventual clarification of right and wrong, of good and evil—the harvest. What form that harvest will take is beyond our knowing.

36

Good can be born of evil

When a tragedy occurs, on either an individual or a mass scale, we usually say, "This is unmitigated evil; why did God let it happen!" Without in the least dampening the negative impact of tragedies, I am aware that even a tragic situation, whether that be one person's cancer or a tsunami that wipes out whole towns, can bring out surprising manifestations of good in the surrounding individuals and community. Many devout believers will interpret great suffering with such words as, "God had a purpose for me (or us) in all this," and proceed to make the most of it, ending up with spiritual growth as a result of tragedy. Some people can find good born out of evil through such a faith.

But I am aware that many people who do not hold such a faith can find good through suffering in another way. Good can be experienced in the way friends or communities respond to suffering with good will and sacrificial deeds of assistance and encouragement. Tragedy brings out the good in us; it calls forth a compassionate spirit that would otherwise lie dormant.

37

Centripetal and centrifugal forces

Evil is the perennial problem! If God is an imminent part of our human nature, then demonic forces also must be of the same nature—immanent and ever present. By "demonic" I do not mean "of the devil" or some objective evil force, but rather the perverseness, the sinister ambivalence of our nature, which drives us in errant directions and can indeed lead to monstrous behavior depending on contextual influences—think of the young men in recent American history who have committed gross multiple murders.

Here is a perspective: the demonic is the *eros*-drive in human nature, and God is the *agape*-drive in human nature. The *eros*-drive is that essential drive for self-preservation such as all living beings have. It is our nature as members of the animal kingdom.

In contrast, the God within is the *agape*-drive, i.e., the drive to go out of myself in creativity and love, a centrifugal force, epitomized by Jesus and his willing death not for what he had done, but for what he was doing for others.

So we are caught in between the centrifugal (God-like) power and the centripetal (self-centered, demonic) power. This puts us in a state of anxiety and confusion. It also makes us feel constantly guilty because we perceive that we *should* be open to the drive toward compassion and charity, but too often are overpowered by the centripetal drive to preserve our self above all else.

38

Observable and non-observable sin

Our ordinary observation of human frailty sees only observable behaviors (the phenomenological aspect). But the Bible sees another dimension (the metaphysical aspect) of sin. In Biblical thought, wrongdoing is primarily seen not as individual misdeeds, but as indifference or hostility toward the Creator of life, and this is not an observable behavior.

Consider the religion of Israel: although it was encumbered with countless ritualistic laws and regulations, at the basis of Israel's faith was this deep awareness of the invisible, spiritual dimension of their sin—their all-too-frequent rejection of Yahweh.

Or consider the attitudes of the religious people of Jesus' day, one of the factors, along with Roman antagonism, that finally nailed him to the cross. The most obvious thing was jealousy, because it seemed to them Jesus was usurping their place of leadership in the religious community, and so they wanted to get rid of this imposter; the people around Jesus were closed, self-serving and defensive instead of willing to be open to a new work of God in their midst. This is the essence of human sinfulness.

39

Built-in judgment

Progressive theology puts much emphasis on a "benevolent universe" and an all-embracing God. Surely that reflects the Gospel. But in this context how are we to think about all that is *not* good in the universe? The title of a book asked, "Whatever Became of Sin?" There is a tendency in progressive theology to overlook the realities of sin, evil and judgment. How do we reconcile all-encompassing divine love with a reckoning for evil-doers? That baffling question is one that has been tossed around since the beginning of time.

Regarding judgment, one clue may be found in Jesus' discourse found in the third chapter of John's Gospel. Consider these words: "God did not send his Son into the world to condemn the world, but to save the world.... but whoever does not believe stands condemned already...Light has come into the world, but.... everyone who does evil hates the light...for fear that his deeds will be exposed."

That is, *we judge ourselves* when we don't open ourselves to the light of the divine presence or to the leading of our conscience. God does not stand over us with a big stick. The struggle goes on in each individual's inner moral structure. Turning our back to the light—to that which is good and honest and loving—is dangerous; it leads to a path of self-destruction, destruction of the neighbor, and to suffering and misery. That suffering is the "built-in" judgment we ought to fear.

40

God—as close as my breath!

Why have human beings of all times and cultures and races always, in some manner, sought after God? That, in spite of the fact that no one has ever even seen God! And we—why do we continue to worship and pray and believe when we have never seen God?

Look at it this way: Our story of creation says "God created human beings in his own image." There is the clue: Our true basic self is something made to resemble God. Therefore, we continually seek our Maker in order to fulfill that image, to find our true self.

And further, many mystical-minded persons seek to identify the self with God. There is both danger and meaning in that. Danger if we come to worship our self as supreme. But on the other hand, if we are made "in the image" of God, that is saying that God is truly in us, a part of our nature. We will not be fulfilled until we realize the divine potential of our nature.

Sometimes in my own pondering about the nature of God, I see a relationship that suggests the identity of God and *life*. Life is the most mysterious and most precious thing we human beings know. If God truly is with us always, then God is right there, creatively involved in life as we know it. God is as close as my breath, yes! And God is in my blood stream, yes! To despise myself is to despise God; to despise God is to despise myself.

41

Living in the *now*

The more I try to be mindfully present in the *now*, the more I realize how exceedingly difficult that is to do! Yet at the same time I realize how exceedingly important it is to do just that. Being present in the *now* requires focused spiritual energy. It seems to take simultaneously a certain abandon and commitment.

The opposite of being fully present in the now is letting my "monkey-mind" take over —that primitive, undisciplined mind that flits about from this thought to that and refuses to focus on the present. It dwells on the past with its scolding, "Too late," filling me with guilt. Or it dwells on the future with its idle dreaming, "Do it later—tomorrow," filling me with unproductive fantasies.

The temptation is to look for a better, more appropriate time to think through things, or to do necessary things, but that time never comes, never will come. Dwelling on the past or the future robs us of reality, robs us of living deeply.

God is beyond time; God is eternal, and today *eternal is revealed as now*. If God, and faith, are not *now experiences*, then they are completely non-existent for me. So revel in eternity—now, I mean *now!*

42

Sin and grace in a nutshell

Two basic concepts in Christian theology and Christian experience are the understandings of sin and of grace. Let me explain what sin and grace mean to me at this point in my spiritual journey.

I believe there is a mysterious Power we usually call "God" which is the source of the universe, the originating power of all creation—our earth and our human selves included. Our mission in life—our reason for existence—is to care for that creation, including air, water, soil, plants, animals and human beings—my being and all beings.

But we fail to fulfill this mission adequately because of our inherent ego-centric nature, which wants only to satisfy our needs and wants and to protect our own self. Actually, this movement of preserving the self is necessary for survival. We have a moral sense which accuses us of not living up to our original mission, our primary calling. Even though it is inevitable, this failure is what we call "sin." Sin is all that is against our highest calling, our fullest potential.

Now for grace. The Christian revelation sees that *God is love*. That is, the author of our life graciously accepts us as we are, even in this bondage to self-centeredness. Through the teachings, life and death of Jesus, God's Messiah, we can know that God forgives us, reconciles us, accepts us, gives us hope. This is grace.

When we awake to the reality that we are indeed acceptable in spite of our sin, at that moment, the only apt response we can make is "Thank you! Thank you! Thank you!"

V

Personal Encounters

If there were not actually some meaningful encounters between God and human beings, there would be no "religious experience." But I share some of my own mystical encounters with God.

43

ESP

Existential religious or spiritual experiences come to me something like this: Without warning an "insight" pops into my awareness. It is not a clear rational idea. Neither is it an emotion, a feeling of joy or awe. It is something between thought and emotion, thinking and feeling. Intuition or new awareness might be the best descriptive. It is literally extra-sensory experience—"ESP" in popular parlance.

There is an unreasoned, spontaneous clarity and conviction about this new awareness. It is more meaningful than the usual learning experience, on a deeper level than the intellect. The content of this intuition is a more profound awareness of the Spirit, self, life, death, and so forth.

It is a momentary experience, and if I do not focus on these nudges of subtle inner movement, this spiritual stirring, and grasp its essence, it flits away like a whiff of perfume. The nudge is like a knock at the door, a door that I must open. It is like a gift, but I must pick it up and open it, appropriate it for myself.

44

Wisps of heaven

Occasionally I have completely unexpected, sudden moments of meaningful experience that are for me little "revelations." For instance, recently while driving the Freeway I turned on the radio and was flooded with beautiful choral music—it was a Sunday morning. Immediately upon hearing it, I was overcome with a spiritual reality, and could only say, This is for me a meeting with the Divine.

Just one moment of pure, exhilarating beauty, whether visual or audible, can be a deeper experience of the divine Mystery, of God, of heaven, than reading tomes of theology. I have found that the spiritual and the esthetic both "speak the same language." And this language can actually hold more meaning than the language of logic.

I am reminded of the words of Simone Weil, "In everything which gives us the pure authentic feeling of beauty there is the presence of God.... The beauty of the world is Christ's tender smile for us, coming through matter."

45

Cell phones and mystery

I am fascinated by the sight of countless numbers of people using their internet and cell phone devices on the street, on the train, in restaurants—wherever! But one day, while waiting on the platform for a train, my eye fell on a young man talking on his device, and something struck me as if for the first time. The realization of what he was doing overwhelmed me: These invisible, everywhere present electronic waves—where are they? What are they? How can it be that this young man is thus conversing with his friend in—who knows where—maybe on the approaching train, maybe in China.

At that moment I thought, If we can experience the mystery of the internet and the cell phone as an everyday reality, why do we have trouble believing the unseen world of spiritual energies? If this fellow can hear his friend coming to him invisibly from afar through the ether waves, surely I can hear the voice of the Spirit coming to me through invisible waves.

Words of adoration and praise come to my lips: O God, invisible, creative Energy of the universe, I stand in awe of the mystery of electronic transmission, the mystery of electric waves, of light waves and of brain waves. The world is submerged in powerful electric waves and emanations and quarks and a host of other invisible powerful emanations too mysterious for me to understand. The explanations of science are too shallow. I am in awe.

46

At Holy Communion

I confess that often participation in the Eucharist at church or elsewhere is no more than a perfunctory ritual. But when I took the Communion wafer at the altar today, as I heard the pastor's words, "The body of Christ given for you," the wafer became so real in my mouth. I tasted and felt that food going into my system was the being of Christ, the Spirit of God. To taste and feel the Presence within me—what a comfort! This surely is a true experience of "sacrament"—a unity of the spiritual and the physical. In John 6 are the words of Jesus, "You must eat me..." Yes, the Christ is here, waiting to be incorporated into my life. That is profound.

47

Is this "revelation"?

Occasionally a mystifying inspiration pops into my consciousness. Should it be called imagination? Or insight? Or revelation? Whatever it is, at some unexpected moments it helps to clarify a "big question" for me. It is not mainly emotional, nor is it the result of reasoning. It is a sudden recognition of a new truth or new perspective that has profound meaning for me. For example:

Today as I was driving down a familiar street—Orange Grove in Pomona—and looked at the tall palm trees in the foreground and the mountains in the background, all of a sudden a deeply meaningful insight overpowered me. Interestingly, I can't put it into words, and if I do it sounds trite, but I was filled with gratitude, and my mind was at rest. What I carried away from that moment goes something like this:

Everything is of one piece. The whole world fits together in harmony. I have a place in this larger scheme, a place which is comfortable, secure. There is an assurance that "all is well," and will come out right. All this constitutes the benevolent huge reality we call God. This total picture is the overwhelming grace of the benevolent Creator. It is the experience of "God

---

48

The unending miracle

Something we are slow to accept is the element of unpredictability in the manner of activity of this divine Presence. As a prime example, we believe that activity was singularly strong in the person of Jesus. We are told that his birth was miraculous. But in a sense, is not every birth a miracle? And, if we dare to tread on delicate ground here, can we not say that resurrection is not necessarily unique to Jesus? There is annual resurrection in the plant kingdom. Likewise, if Jesus could be resurrected, so can we, as he himself said we will be.

Seeing Jesus primarily as being God or "Son of God" has the effect of setting Jesus apart as a kind of superman or magical person. The divine Spirit was indeed incarnated in an amazing way in this man Jesus. But the counterpart of that is that the same divine Spirit can be incarnated in every person in a way unique to that person. This radical understanding flows directly from Jesus' frequent repetition of the words (in John's Gospel): "I in them, Thou in me, that we may all be one."

49

Resting under "the easy yoke"

"No one knows the Father except the Son and those to whom the Son chooses to reveal him" (Matt. 11.27) are strange words. But I believe what they say is that we don't find God—no matter how hard we try to figure out God—by reason and ritual. Rather, it is God who reveals God's self to us.

The saying continues: "Come to me all you who are burdened, and I will give you rest. Take my yoke upon you...and you will find rest for your souls..." Straining to find God through, for example, academic or philosophical machinations (as I am wont to do!) is the "burden," whereas simply "resting" in God—simple, child-like trusting—is the "easy yoke." "Anyone who will not receive the kingdom of God like a little child will never enter it." (Mark10)

50

Open up!

The almost spontaneous prayer from human lips in time of need is, "God, be with me and help me!" But that is not a proper prayer, for God is *always* with and in human beings. We can't escape God even if we try. So why do we tend to say, God, be with me? Probably because we are vaguely aware that we are not in touch with this divine Spirit as we might be.

Is it not more appropriate to say, "God, make me *aware* of your presence; let me be open to the gifts you offer"? In other words, although there is no need to ask someone who is already present to come and be with us, nevertheless, we do need to open the door for the Spirit knocking there if we are to appropriate that "help."

Sadly, our human nature is to leave that door closed. It seems automatically to pull back in "closed" position unless there is some gesture on our part to keep it open. But, here is an amazing thing—there are times when the divine grace overwhelms us even when we utterly fail to open the gate.

Recognizing the constant presence of God, there is no need to moan, I am so miserable; God has forsaken me! No, why not say, "Lord, as you know, here's what's happening with me now; what shall we do about it? I'm glad you are with me in this mess; let's find the best way to handle it!"

51

Nothing has changed, but…..

Riding the ferry from Larkspur to San Francisco we were in the usual cloud of fog until we got to the middle of the Bay. Then suddenly the fog lifted to unveil beautiful blue skies and the magnificent San Francisco skyline—the surprise of what seemed like a new, wonderful world! What had happened? Nothing had changed, but everything was different.

This is the paradox of our finding God nowhere, leaving a bleak, cold universe, or finding God everywhere, turning a bland life into a joyful life.

Another analogy is that of being in a dark room, unaware of the fine furnishings in the room. Then we turn the lights on and everything changes—though nothing has changed! What has changed is a new awareness of the environment, an awareness of beauty where there had been darkness. I think faith is like that—it gives us new eyes, new vision.

52

The inner dialogue

I experience an inner awareness that is a kind of dialogue between my conscious self and another Self—a dialogue that is always comforting and supportive. It is the experience of the Other which knows me better than I know myself. It is always a positive impetus toward clarifying a difficult situation or making a right decision. It is one of the everyday, practical benefits of having an intimate relationship with that Other which/whom we call God.

This dialogue is, I think, what Christians traditionally call "hearing and responding to the Word of God." But it can also be described in other ways, and experienced through other channels. For instance, it is similar to an inner dialogue with my "higher self" such as Psychosynthesis teaches. Or it is also similar to the experience of writing Progoff Journal dialogues, an opportunity provided at a Jesuit retreat center in the Bay Area, which was greatly beneficial to me.

The Inscrutable One does indeed work in mysterious ways—ways beyond conventional, orthodox, Christian creedal, doctrinal definitions.

53

I am God's possession

During an angina attack at night I fearfully imagined, "Could this be the end? Am I ready?" Then there came a strong wave I can describe only as a "religious experience." A "point" appeared; a literal big dot became inwardly visible to me. From it emanated a voice that said confidently, "You are the possession of God! You do not possess yourself. God made you, so God possesses you and takes responsibility for you. God gave you birth; God will take you in death. What is there to worry about!"

This "vision" gave me relief from anxiety about death and I went to sleep. The whole thing was dream-like, but whether it was a conscious experience or an unconscious one, it was a revelation of a truth that I want to hold precious for the rest of my life.

VI

Nurturing the Links Between spirit and Spirit

What are some things we can do to nurture our spiritual life so that we remain in touch with the divine Spirit?

54

What is my role?

If truly "all is of grace," what then is my role in the spiritual pilgrimage? We say grace is the divine action working on us from beyond our self, and faith is our subjective appropriation of grace. Grace is God's doing; faith involves my will and effort. But we also claim that faith itself is a gracious gift. So is there nothing we can do?

What is *my part* in the human/divine encounter? In my tradition, the role of personal faith tends to be smothered by the constant emphasis on "Salvation is entirely by grace; there is nothing we can do." One of my seminary professors maintained adamantly that "You cannot even say Yes to God; the best we can do is to stop saying No." Hmm. But the shibboleth is not only *sola gratia*, but also *sola fide*. So how can I act out my faith?

Just as a starter, we could begin with a very practical answer, an everyday practice. I show my faith when I actually set aside time to hear and recognize the Spirit at work in my life. And I can—must—do the necessary mental discipline of focusing my mind on the grace and goodness of God; that is not something God does for me.

St. Paul said, "Work out your own salvation." This is not a cancellation of "justification by faith." I believe it is saying that each of us has to work to discover the meaning of the divine activity in our own life.

55

Essential quiet time

It is no wonder that there are myriads of techniques for spending quiet time efficaciously, within both Christian and non-Christian circles. Times of quiet reflection, meditation, contemplation, etc. are absolutely necessary for seeking and adventuring into that realm of the spirit, which is the highest potential of human beings. We may call it "prayer," or "spirituality," or "Zen meditation," etc. All of these recognize that there is something more to our life than what is obvious and constantly bombarding us through the five senses. That something goes by such names as the *"More"* or the *"Other"* of our human experience, or *Spirit*—these being the lowest common denominator for what most of us call *"God."*

It takes a certain focus, a listening attitude, a quiet mind to recognize, to be aware of these complex, mysterious whispers or insights that give us an experience of Spirit. The mind and heart are as complicated and wonderful as the physical body, or as the unfathomable universe.

How do we get in touch with our core spirit which links us to the Spirit? Paul Tillich often said that we can't understand *Spirit* until we understand *spirit*. How do we cultivate our own spirit? For most people, that is in quiet time. We each must find our own path into solitude, where extra-sensory vistas can open up to us.

56

The spirit-flesh struggle

I experience this old conflict in a very internal way—the Spirit is always surrounding me, and is in me, but my flesh prohibits me from being aware of this. The biblical concept of "flesh" is much broader than sensuality or lust; it includes everything that omits the Spirit. My natural state is to set my mind on the myriad of things occupying my thinking, feeling and awareness that constantly cloud over the spiritual.

So what is required of us is to pierce the cloud by means of various "spiritual disciplines," e.g., prayers, mindfulness, meditation. Prayer is the window which opens to let the Spirit to rush into our awareness. (The Hebrew word for "spirit"—*ruach*— also means "wind.") The natural inclination to focus on material and sensate things, being indifferent to the call of God, is a manifestation of the spirit-flesh struggle, a manifestation of what is traditionally called "original sin."

57

There is no tomorrow

These fantastically beautiful snow-capped mountains
    I will feel their majesty—tomorrow
These crimson red, orange and yellow leaves of the liquidambar tree
    I will relish their beauty—tomorrow
This relationship bursting with possibilities for happy times together,
    I'll enjoy it—tomorrow
The awesome Creator of the universe,
    I'll worship this One—tomorrow.
Then time ended for me
    I went where there is no time
No time but now, and I realized that
    Tomorrow never came and
Sadly, I had never lived
    because I never knew how
    to live in the now.

58

The Vertical Dimension

Karen Armstrong and other contemporary voices are claiming that the essence of religion, of all true faith in any religion, regardless of their recognition or non-recognition of a god or God, is *compassion*. This may be close to the truth, but for me it is not the whole picture. It is great for an ethical principle, but it lacks the vertical dimension, which makes religion be religion.

Jesus taught this about the essence of religion: "The greatest commandment is to love the Lord your God with all your heart and soul and mind." In the Old Testament writings there is constant repetition of the phrase, "They shall know that I am God." We cannot escape the vertical dimension, the fundamental importance of this recognition of and hallowing of the Mystery we call "God."

Compassion, the horizontal dimension of spirituality—"Love your neighbor as yourself"—comes as the second great commandment.

59

We live by trust

Look at the cars on the freeways—literally millions of them driving at high speed, within inches of each other, day and night. It's amazing there are not more traffic accidents than there are. Why? Because we drive *trusting* each other to keep in one lane and not veer to the right or left, to observe the rules of the road, to practice common sense. *Trust* is that purely invisible spiritual sense that allows us to use highways and freeways and thus maintain modern urbanized culture. Of course there is the occasional accident, but that's another story!

This is an allegory of our life as a whole. We live it in trust of the One who is the source of all life. We can trust that One, because God has shown—in nature, in history, and especially in the person of Jesus—the divine self as being generous and loving, not in the sense of delivering us from all misfortunes, but to give hope no matter what happens. Knowing that and trusting in the source of that hope, we are free to live without fear.

60

Using the Lord's Prayer

When I want to pray but don't know what to say, I turn to the Lord's Prayer. But rather than saying the traditional standard words, I substitute other contemporary words that the original words and phrases mean for me at this time. For instance, "Our" becomes "God of all people, and God of myself;" "Father" becomes "Loving Source of all life;" "hallowed" becomes "I honor you and bow before your mystery." "Thy Kingdom come" becomes "Let us recognize your lordship over all of life, my life and the life of our nation and all nations," and so forth through the entire prayer.

In that prayer, we pray, "Lead us not into temptation." What temptation? Tempted to do what? Put this question in the context of the other petitions of the prayer, and we can understand temptation referring to the negative side of all the positive petitions—the content of the first part of the prayer.

Looking at it that way, the "temptations" refer to forgetting the holy presence of God ("hallowed be thy name"), to forget the invisible Kingdom of love and justice ("thy Kingdom come"), to worry about only our own daily necessities ("give *us* our *daily* bread"), or to harbor resentment rather than maintaining a forgiving attitude ("forgive us as we forgive others").

These temptations are more insidious in the long run than what we usually think of as temptation, such as the temptation to indulge our lustful desires. They reach to our life in society, as well as our own inner life.

66

VII

How Then Are We to Act?

What manner of behavior should characterize the person who tries to live a Christian life?

61

An inseparable duo

Where does the faith-life lie—in the heart or in one's behavior? In neither. It must lie in the correlation of the two—the thought and the deed. If it is only in the "heart," it is a mere abstraction, a fleeting concept of the brain. If it is only in action, it becomes a legalistic external show.

Thinking a prayer is not enough. Thoughts of piety, commitment and trust in God must issue in a life stance. I love God by loving my neighbor.

A bi-polar view, with the possibility of a bridge between the poles of "roots and fruits" is a needed message for our community in Claremont. The *roots* pole is biblical faith, and the *fruits* pole is social action for justice and peace in the world. There is a general tendency to emphasize one at the expense of the other.

But there needs to be a bridge between the two, so they are not in conflict, but are complementary, two halves that compose one whole. These two should be combined like root and branch, or branch and fruit. Our retirement community, Pilgrim Place, is strong on the *fruit* pole, while most evangelical churches are strong on the *root* pole. We need a view that encompasses both poles. Not to have this ends up, at the extremes, with piety in a vacuum or with a secular social program.

62

Who wants to sacrifice!

Is there anything Americans loathe to do more than *sacrifice*, or even to accept sacrifice as a value? Maybe that's one good thing about military service—troops have to be prepared to sacrifice themselves for a cause they believe to be greater than themselves.

Sacrifice, ironically, is at the very heart of Christian belief and living. An unpopular, paradoxical saying of Jesus is, "Whoever wants to save his life will lose it, but whoever loses his life for me will save it." (Luke 9) We glorify the sacrifice of Christ, and we hold that our life must be patterned after his, i.e., the road of sacrificing self for others. But the truth is that this way of life seems to have gone way off the horizon of modern Americans, with our exaltation of prosperity and success.

63

The moral code

The revelation of God to the Jewish people was that the true God was not any visible "thing" to be worshipped, but was the giver of a moral code to be obeyed. Thus the highest object of reverence for the Jews was the Ten Commandments and the other parts of the Law, the Torah.

What this means for me is that to honor the true God, and Jesus the Messiah, the Son, I should not focus on any visible object or on religious rituals. Rather, I focus on the Commandments, and how to keep them rightly. What that means for my daily pilgrimage is that I am in a constant inner dialogue with that font of morality, asking myself, Am I doing the right thing, the thing I ought to be doing this week, this day, this hour? Are my actions in line with what Jesus taught as the greatest commandment, the law of love? Or have I gotten on a side track?

At the beginning of each day we would do well to take time out to establish orientation and perspective on what we believe will be the right use of time and energy for that day. We should set our moral compass afresh daily, determining what the priorities for that day should be. These matters can become the substance of our prayers.

64

What is there about Sunday?

It is strange that "Keep the Sabbath" should be one of the primary commandments according to Jewish-Christian morality. Why should that be an important point of the moral code set forth in the Ten Commandments, on a par with "Do not kill"?

I think that the Sabbath, in addition to offering needed physical rest, symbolizes a time set aside to remember our origins, to remember what is ultimately important for us, to contemplate the meaning and goals of our life. How important it is to have reminders of these spiritual values, lest we so easily drown in material things and get lost in daily work routines. Yes, "keeping the Sabbath" is a vital moral obligation. For many of us that means attending church, but we must grant that there are also other ways to keep the Sabbath.

65

A common ground for all religions

The obvious fact about human existence is that we human beings did not create either the universe or ourselves. Putting this in religious terms, we say that all things—from quarks to galaxies—are not the product of human achievement, but are a given fact of life. Yes, a *given*; they are *gifts!* Therefore, the most becoming attitude for all persons is grateful humility and gratitude, while the least becoming attitude is arrogance.

The primary importance of this stance speaks to interfaith issues. People of all religious beliefs can take as their starting point this common ground of humble gratitude before the Giver of Life in all its wonderful diversity.

66

We're all part of the puzzle

We should view all things, including our own self, as links in a long chain, or, to change the metaphor, as pieces in a jig-saw puzzle. Each of us, like those pieces, has a different size, shape and color, so to speak. That is, from the perspective of the whole of society, each of us fits with all others, and each has a different role, a function to fulfill. This function is for the common good, for the sake of harmony and balance of the whole group, or community, or society. Recall St. Paul's analogy of the body and its members.

When one individual, one part of the whole, usurps privileges that belong to everyone, or uses other persons or things for his or her own satisfaction at the expense of others, rather than letting each carry out their own function freely, the balance is upset, and the common good is destroyed. When this happens on a broad scale, the situation slips into injustice, and then oppression, and that is what we call sin, social sin, sin which destroys both individuals and society.

67

Make daily life richer

Accept your acceptance. Remember that the Author of your life accepts you as you are, because that One who made you loves you. You are, as Martin Luther was wont to say, a "forgiven sinner." And forgiveness is not past-oriented, as in "I did a bad thing yesterday so I need God's forgiveness."

Rather, it is a continuous process. There is much undone, omitted, neglected, so much imperfection in every part of my daily thoughts, words and deeds. If I have a morally sensitive conscience, I feel guilt and berate myself for this. But at that moment I remind myself that my slate can be cleaned many times a day—"seventy times seven" to quote the parable of Jesus, so that I can say, "I am forgiven, even now at this moment. I can make a fresh start *now*." This allows me to go forward thanking God for this unmerited "acceptance-in-spite-of."

Strive for mindfulness, for *awareness.* Mindfulness is not simply being passively aware of what's going on around us. It is, so to speak, putting adjectives and adverbs on to what we are observing, i.e., recognizing the special nature of what the senses are bringing to us, evaluating what we see and experience, and recognizing the ethical and also the esthetic dimensions of what we are experiencing. Then we respond to what we're aware of, by being either critical of or thankful for this experience, evaluating it, and responding to it. This stance makes every day sparkle with meaning and discovery.

VIII

As I See It: a Potpourri

My reflections turn toward a miscellany of a few of my own observation and experiences, sacred and secular.

68

Non-verbal expressions of faith

It is very difficult to be precise in articulating Christian faith, because God remains a mystery that cannot be rationally explained, and also because our response to God is subjective and thus different for every person.

So if reason and rational language are not adequate for expressing matters of faith, we can try to use non-verbal means of expression. One of those means is art.

Artistic expression includes a wide range of endeavors, including audio arts (music), visual arts (painting, sculpture, architecture, etc.), drama (theater), literature, etc.—these are avenues for expressing inner feelings, intuition and convictions that constitute our faith and give form to it.

Perhaps one of the prime examples of this is the medieval cathedrals found in Europe. The architecture itself, and the plethora of art within the building, expressed the faith of otherwise illiterate folk of the time. Their creeds were expressed through stained glass windows, murals, and much more.

My own efforts in artistic expression have been very limited but meaningful, at least to myself. Through piano music I have tried to express an intuitive or emotional grasp of God's majesty and mysterious surprises. And in later years, in painting I have tried to express something of the mystery of the Creator through abstract expressionism.

69

"Order and Chaos"

It was a great satisfaction to be able to open an exhibition of my work in painting at a gallery in Claremont in August, 2013. The theme I chose was "Order and Chaos." My statement posted for that exhibition read as follows:

"I see life, both on the individual and social plane, as a mixture of order and chaos—never completely ordered, never completely in chaos. This speaks to me of the peace of God in the midst of human turmoil. Here I attempt to express this reality through intuitive, non-verbal means of expression rather than through rational, verbal expression. Notice that there is a degree of both orderly and random arrangement of shapes and colors in the composition of these paintings.

Just as there is something beautiful in the harmonies and dissonances that make music delight our ear, so we hopefully find something of beauty in the shapes and colors of these paintings that are in themselves fingers pointing to inexpressible feeling, quite apart from any object they might represent.

Of course, communication through art, as through most non-verbal communication, necessarily lacks precision. It is suggestive rather than definitive; it appeals to imagination rather than to reason. It leaves us with questions, and maybe a sense of mystery—or of the Mystery."

70

The powerful message of the senses

We fail too often to be grateful for the contribution of the five senses. The senses in and of themselves, without words, produce emotional impact that can create meaning for the whole person. It doesn't need the interpretive work of the intellect. It can produce meaningful experience as effectively as the mind does. When we hear the finale of a great symphony, see a fantastic red sunset, or smell the fragrance of blooming jasmine, etc., there is no need to analyze what the senses are bringing to awareness and run it through the filter of mental cogitation. They can relay esthetic experience and meaning directly to our inner spirit. We need only to be thankful for them!

These strong sensory experiences are the human *eros* at work. *Eros* has a way of fully occupying the attention and communicating meaning. We can simply let it speak without encumbering it with reasoning. Consider the pinnacle experience of eros—sexual orgasm, where the pleasure of the senses becomes absolutely compelling. This is *eros* at its highest strength; therefore, we call such experiences "erotic."

Sensory experience as such is morally neutral, but it is nevertheless an indispensable element of human life, and is a cause for gratitude, not suppression.

71

A new metaphor

I have discovered a new metaphor or analogy by which to think about the experience of the divine Spirit at work in our everyday life—the analogy with sexuality. Although this insight is new to me, mystics throughout the ages have used sexual imagery to describe their deep spiritual experiences.

Let's say that your body is tired, bored, without any feeling or joy. Then you are stimulated either by internal or external stimuli to turn your mind to the pleasure of sexual activity. There quickly arises within you a whole new array of feelings. Whereas you had been cold and lifeless, you now feel excitement and joy—a transformation of the total self.

And where did all this energy come from? It was not external energy, it was an internal energy. The potential for it was there all the time, just waiting to be aroused to work this remarkable transformation.

The analogy to spiritual deadness and spiritual arousal to joy and hope is obvious. I focus here on the manner of this "awakening" which is a latent, hidden potential in our body and soul, which can be awakened by some inner experience, or by an outer stimulus such as hearing a powerful sermon or reading words of Scripture. Even though we hold to the mystery of *grace*, the gifts of God are not something simply handed to us on a platter from above. In one sense I believe these gifts of grace, contrary to doctrines of "total depravity," are latent potential within our own selfhood—the latent "image of God" within us.

72

On the "Truth of Cause"

In Buddhism, one of the "Four Noble Truths" is the "Truth of Cause" (*jittai*). This is an important aspect of ethical living which seems not to have found a place in the usual structures of Christian theology. But it is a truth of the moral sphere which we might well borrow from Buddhism and utilize in the Christian view of life.

That is, *jittai* looks for the causal factor of any problem before fretting about the problem itself. It works on cause, not effects. Applying this to our current social or international situation, this would usually get at issues of justice rather than simply aiming to, say, eradicate hunger by doling out food, or by trying to eradicate terrorists in the Middle East by killing them one by one.

But it seems we hesitate to point out causes for the social problems that face us, because that is often upsetting to a larger system, to the establishment, in which all of us are engulfed. It is unfortunately true that when people work for short term relief from obvious problems that are recognizable to all, they are hailed as heroes. But ironically, when they work on the roots of injustice that lie behind those problems they are too often condemned as left-wing radicals. We need to learn the lesson of *jittai!*

73

An experience of healing

On a Sunday noon while driving home from Fontana, where I had been in charge of the service, I felt a strong leading to pray that the intense arthritic pain in the fingers of my right hand would be relieved. I held my right hand up to the windshield and said, "God, send your healing power to these fingers." Almost instantly I felt much better and almost no pain in my fingers for the rest of that day.

That finger was usually so stiff and painful in the morning that I hardly dared to clench my fingers and test them the next morning. But as I did so, there was, miraculously, no pain at all. Since then there has been much less pain than before—a vast change! I am in awe!

74

Resolving differences

Controversy and division are plaguing our churches. We have sharp differences regarding biblical interpretation and ethical behavior and political positions. And so we feel resentful and denigrate each other. We become alienated and stand in opposing camps throwing stones at each other. Finally we say, "You're not a true Christian, so we can't fellowship with you. We're going to start our own group."

This is so regrettable, so wrong! We have a responsibility to discuss and debate issues in order to come to the best conclusions about problems. We have no right to condemn each other or accuse each other of not being Christian, just because they have contrary points of view. To do so violates Jesus' teaching on not judging, and it is destructive to the community.

Rather, we must say to each other, "We have deep differences in our thinking, but we both trust the same God, believe in the same Christ and follow the same Holy Spirit. Let's maintain our fellowship in faith and agree that for now we disagree about certain issues, but that need not alienate us from each other. Let us take it as a challenge to work toward mutual understanding." The adage, "Let's agree to disagree," can be a profound, reconciliatory statement.

75

Old Testament Nationalism

I Chronicles 17 relates King David's rise to power. His prayer is utterly nationalistic, his idea of Israel thoroughly theocratic. How are we to understand this narrow view of the Old Testament, which constantly sees God as only the God of the Jews, sees Palestine as God's special land for Israel, foretells the eternal greatness of the Kingdom of Israel? This is the dilemma of Israel!

The writers of the history of Israel had limited vision. They did not have broad insight into any larger plan for the world. But we are all bound by our historical, contextual limitations, and wear blinders to the larger dimensions of a future we cannot predict.

We all want to think that God is, or ought to be, especially favoring and blessing *us*. No person can ever grasp the scope of the total "will of God." This behooves us to be tolerant of world-views and political systems different from ours, and to see our own national interests in the context of the entire family of nations, and in terms of centuries of global development rather than in terms of one nation's immediate success, which can be the root of ultra-nationalism.

76

"I'm sorry"

Upon returning from decades of living in Japan, we have become acutely aware, to our dismay, that Americans, in striking contrast to the Japanese, are typically unapologetic. The examples are innumerable, but this is a recent one.

When our plane out of O'Hare in Chicago was two and a half hours late arriving in Denver, causing us to miss our night flight from there to our destination, causing us the great inconvenience of having to stay overnight in a hotel, no one in all that process, neither flight attendants nor airline representatives at counters, ever offered a word of apology or any acknowledgement of our plight. Only the pilot, when we finally took off from O'Hare after two and a half hours on the tarmac, mumbled something about causing inconvenience.

I know we are spoiled by Japanese extreme politeness, but "I'm sorry" goes a long way in any culture to soothe agitated or ruffled feelings. Is it fear of litigation that makes Americans resist apologizing? There seems to be a fear that to apologize is to admit wrong-doing, and that puts one in the vulnerable position of possibly being sued or becoming the "criminal." This is most unfortunate.

I lament this lack of common courtesy and kindness between business personnel and the public, as well as lack of feeling in personal interactions.

77

God as *absconditus* and *revelatus*

In traditional theological vocabulary, God's nature is described as "*absconditus*" (hidden) and "*revelatus*" (revealed). The revelation that Christians know is through the prophets and Jesus. The question in the inter-faith dialogue is, Does that mean this is the *only* revelation?

Let us admit that we finite beings can never know what "*Deus absconditus*" is doing. The hidden God might well be willing a revelation to other planets, and to other cultures and religions in our world today. Our job is not to know or judge what the hidden God is doing. Our job is to follow the revelation that has been given to us—which is the life and teachings and death of Jesus of Nazareth, fulfilling a God-given mission to serve humanity, and the implications that go with that, i.e., "Love one another as I have loved you."

IX

Approaching the End

Finally I share some thoughts, recorded at different stages of my life, on the meaning of growing older, experiencing retirement, and facing the end of life.

78

Symptoms of Aging

I am experiencing the changes in my body and mind that age is bringing upon me. Tiring easily, forgetting words, forgetting what I said a week ago—these are a constant phenomena. But beyond that I realize my mind is not as agile as it used to be. Multiple tasking and handling complex situations cause me undue anxiety. I often have to read long sentences twice to get the meaning straight. When playing the piano, my fingers don't find the right keys as easily as they used to; "muscle memory" is getting impaired. When I am relaxing, I find it a little easier just to let my mind go blank rather than deal with a bundle of thoughts.

As we age we would do well to set attainable goals instead of ideal goals for ourselves. This is the only way to have hope and encouragement in our struggle with increasing limitations. We can focus on just this day, just this one act, and let concrete "lesser" goals be our guide. It is no longer appropriate to set up ideals of all-or-nothing-at-all, which cause us either to despair before starting or despair at the end when we see we're not up to an over-sized task we had set for ourselves. We must remember St. Paul's words of wisdom, "In whatever state I am, I have learned to be content." (Philippians 4)

79

The burden of health maintenance

Taking care of our various physical ailments—from cataract removals to broken neck surgery and a host of lesser problems calling for medical attention—this seems to absorb all our time and attention these days. My wife Eloise and I spend our time going to appointments with doctors and nurses, waiting in medical offices, undergoing hospitalization routines, spending our money on drugs, treatments and doctors. Our energy is spent on maintaining our health, maintaining the physical body —or in cynical moments I am tempted to say, spending our time and resources just prolonging the dying process. Is this the way we must spend our later years?

80

Retirement--a wasteland?

I've been retired for six months, but it's clear that, in this strange new world of retirement, I haven't yet established a new identity. At the feeling level I still am a professor at Japan Lutheran College and Seminary. Not to be able to say that leaves an uncomfortable, gaping hole. I hate to write on the "Occupation" line in documents "Retired," and cross out "Work Place" and "Profession." How shall I learn to live comfortably in this new reality of retirement?

This feels like a wasteland, where I hear a nagging voice, "You've become detached. Where are you going from now on?" I can't hear the Spirit's voice of hope, but I call out anyway and beg for God's presence, for without that the future is a blank wall.

This is not really depression, but perhaps should be called "retirement blues." I realize that emotionally as well as rationally my life has been defined by my work, which was so challenging and fulfilling. It demanded response and responsibility. It gave me a place, a status among peers. Now that rug has been pulled out from under me. There is an urgency about setting up a new framework, a new world-view.

81

When can I let myself retire?

I'm experiencing a kind of "lostness" similar to what I experienced after retirement. Both then and now I'm having a different daily routine, one with loss of specific schedule and tasks that I've been used to. Now it is because I feel a change in energy level. I tire more easily; I need to rest after a few hours of exertion; I need a nap most days, and I need 8-9 hours of sleep at night.

Because of these facts, I'm resigning from several areas of work that have been satisfying in the past, such as volunteering at the Botanic Gardens and at the Food Pantry. I'm also trying to be relieved of some committee work. I realize that I'm not indispensable, and that "the younger ones" (the 60 and 70-year-olds!) are there to take over. This gives me a little more free time than I have ever known in the past, and that is wonderful. Perhaps in my 80's I am allowing myself to retire at last!

82

A new way of life

After the first decade of retirement I am beginning to feel like a horse that had been in a harness hitched to a wagon and driver all its life, and then suddenly freed of the harness, not knowing what to do with itself. All this unscheduled time! This monthly pension payment without working! The opportunity to choose what I *want* to do, not what I *have* to do!

God grant that the latter years of my life will not be a dead end but a gate on the journey which opens up to a bold new adventure. The outward journey with its work and social involvement and church leadership are behind me.

God, give me a new vision for a new kind of service; give me your Holy Spirit that my spirit may be enriched, deepened and clarified. May I close the curtain on external labels and open a new curtain into my essential self. Grant that I may find the meaning of and contentment with *being*, not just *doing*.

83

How I experienced life at 40

Around age 40 I wrote in a journal: Life at 40 means, for me, rejecting youthful optimism regarding myself and my work, lowering my ideal, expecting less from life. It means accepting my situation for what it actually is, without daily frustration stemming from unrealistic idealism. It also means making a new start, with a new set of values based on this new reality.

Have I sold myself short? Have I given up on life as a bad job and forgotten the recreating power of the Spirit? I believe it means that I have come to emotional maturity by truly accepting and declaring that I am willing to live as a very imperfect person, and that I can accept the realities of my situation without denial or resentment.

84

How I experienced life at 60

Around age 60 I wrote: Since some months before my 60th birthday this spring I have been thinking almost compulsively about retirement and the changes in life style which that will bring, but I am coming to terms with what a year ago seemed an absurd and dreadful fate, namely, that I would actually soon be in the decade of "old age"—my 60's! But after dialoging with myself and with friends about that reality over a period of months, I have now adjusted to feeling fairly comfortable with the facts.

I also feel a release from the need to hang on to middle age, and even from the need to hang on to life itself. It has been a full and worthwhile life, and I have accomplished enough for one little human being.

85

How I experienced life at 70

Around age 70 I wrote: I am thinking seriously about the phenomenon of aging, although I have no sense of "feeling old." The big issues cluster around retirement—where to live (Japan or the U. S.?), what kind of home (independent house or a retirement community?), and most of all, how will I spend my time (in similar work to my career or find a new arena of work?) These are huge issues.

At this stage I have several causes for deep gratitude. I sense the attainment of broader and more balanced perspectives. I feel more tolerant of differing religious beliefs. I feel more indignation toward injustices in society and the world. I am grateful for a caring wife and two sons, and for the support and joy of having the respect and companionship of many colleagues and friends. I feel a calm faith, not so fluctuating and emotional as earlier, but more firm and earthy.

On the other hand I have several anxieties about aging. I feel a number of health problems. I fear the loss of respect and being taken seriously if I am seen as an old man; I fear if I seek other work I will be rejected because of being too old. I dislike the appearance of my aging body—its wrinkles, spots on the skin, thinning, graying hair and more.

86

How I experienced life at 80

Around age 80 I wrote: "I have become an old man"—I want to deny this statement. It is weighted with so much meaning. It has a kind of cosmic significance to me, this admitting that I am now in the later years of my life, that I am indeed an "old man."

Why this feeling? Because there is something radically profound for the meaning of my very existence to admit that this thing called *my life*, the life of Kenneth Dale, born into the Johnson family in Mead, Nebraska, educated as a Lutheran minister, married to Eloise for 66 years and together raised two sons—Gregory and Ted, who lived 45 years in Japan in kinship with Asian people and culture, now retired in Claremont, California—this life is now close to the finish. This pastor, teacher and leader, who has been swimming in a sea of activities since ordination in 1951—this one has now finished his work and is an *old man*, out of the mainstream of life, ready to be put on the shelf by society. Can it be? Yes, it is true.

87

How I experience life at 90

In this, my 90th year, I can share the meaning of my life in a highly abbreviated fashion something like this:

To know that I am in harmony with the God who has sustained my life from birth through 90 years;

To know Jesus Christ who was and is the key to fulfilled humanity;

To enjoy and strengthen the ties among my family;

To maintain friendships and work with people on worthy projects;

To empathize with and help in whatever small way I can peoples of the world who suffer from violence of all kinds, and from injustices in the social order;

To try to understand the struggles of persons around me and help them attain peace;

To discover new depths of theological understanding, and share them as broadly as feasible in a way that has relevance for everyday life;

To enjoy and express myself through music and painting;

To care for my increasingly vulnerable body.

I think these challenges are enough to give me zest for living for perhaps a few more years, God willing!

88

All is one

Science teaches us that material existence is composed of atoms, and each atom is a complex system of *energy*. The ocean, the air, rocks and soil, all plants and animals—and my body—these are all manifestations of different arrangement of atoms, each of which is a bundle of energy. This energy consists of electrons, protons, quarks, "god particles," or whatever the latest scientific discovery leads us to find as the essential building blocks of the universe.

It is virtually impossible to wrap our minds around this concept, for it tells us that there are really no boundaries within the universe. As Richard Rohr repeatedly emphasizes, "All is one; we are all one." This leads me to think differently about my relation to nature. It should compel all of us in the human family to let go of a bit of our arrogance and feeling of superiority.

When we die, perhaps the atoms and electrons, and "god particles" that composed our bodies just dissolve back into the great unity of God and God's creation.

89

When I come to the end

If, when I am near my end, lying in a nursing home, no longer able to contribute anything positive to others, not able to enjoy or be grateful for life, then the least I can do is to avoid being a burden on others and on society. So helping to end my life by refraining from eating would be a worthy, noble and charitable thing to do. It would be my last act of care for others, a completely ethical way of ending life here and returning to the loving Source out of which my life evolved in the beginning.

At the memorial service for a beloved woman of our community, it was mentioned by several people that she had courageously and humbly chosen to end her life. This fact was celebrated in her service. She said that at age 86 she had so many ailments and so much pain that she felt she had suffered enough, and that she had used up enough of the world's resources trying to maintain her life. She said that her body was telling her, "You've had enough of this life; now it's time to go on to the next stage."

In view of this she had simply stopped eating and drinking, and within about ten days her wish to move on was fulfilled. The community was with her supportively throughout her final journey.

90

Pondering the meaning of it all

We begin in the disciplined classroom
    Practicing diligently to play our role heroically
Ah, at last we're out there under the lights;
    The lines go well, the audience applauds
    We work so hard to maintain our reputation.
Later new performers arrive;
    We step back to the sidelines, applauding our colleagues
    As they take over the roles we once played.
Finally we retire to a balcony seat
    And feel nostalgia as we fondly remember
    What it was like to be playing down there on the stage.
The house lights dim; the stage grows dark.
    The play is over, the auditorium is empty.
I go out in the darkness
    Pondering the meaning of it all.

(Revision of my poem published in the Pilgrim Place booklet,
"The Poetry of Aging" (2014))

Made in the USA
Las Vegas, NV
13 February 2022

43843916R00062